# Introduction

This book is about a bloodthirsty and often terrifying period of British history, when the nation was divided and at war with itself and a number of countries in Europe. The Great Plague killed at least one fifth of the people of London and a great fire destroyed much of the city. There was even a plot to blow up the Houses of Parliament!

As much as a tenth of the population of Britain may have been killed in the Civil War, which was fought between King Charles I and the army of Parliament. Charles was defeated and for the first time in British history the nation was not ruled by a king or queen. This did not last very long, but never again was a monarch to rule with absolute power.

This period also saw fantastic advances in scientific knowledge and the creation of some of the most beautiful art and architecture. Our book begins when the King of Scotland, James VI, became King of England.

# Contents

| | Page |
|---|---|
| Stuart Kings and Queens | 3 |
| Daily Life | 5 |
| The Gunpowder Plot | 7 |
| The English Civil War | 9 |
| Oliver Cromwell | 11 |
| The Great Plague | 13 |
| The Great Fire of London | 15 |
| William of Orange | 17 |
| The Arts and Sciences | 19 |
| Giant Stuart Word Search | 21 |
| Timeline and Glossary | 22 |

Written & illustrated by William Webb
Front cover illustration by Les Ives
Published by Colour History Ltd © 2007
Print reference number 28464/10/07

# Stuart Kings & Queens

**The first Stuart monarch was Robert II of Scotland (1316-1390), Robert the Bruce's grandson. He was known as 'the Steward', which is where the family name comes from. When Elizabeth I died in 1603 her closest relative was a Stuart, James VI of Scotland.**

### James I (1603-1625)

James came to the Scottish throne aged just one year old when his mother, Mary Queen of Scots, was arrested for marrying a man the Scottish nobles disliked. Someone ruled on his behalf until he was fifteen. James knew he was likely to become King of England and he sought the favour of all the right people, including Elizabeth I, the Pope and English Catholics.

*James I and his wife, Anne of Denmark*

After he was crowned James I of England, he had to ask Parliament for money in order to wage wars. This made him unpopular with Parliament. England was undergoing change by the Puritans, who were aiming to remove all Roman Catholic traditions from the church. James was a Protestant so he was not opposed to the Puritans, but after the Gunpowder Plot (see page 7) he disliked Catholics. He ordered a new translation of the Bible, which is now known as the King James Bible. He joined other Protestants to fight Catholic Spain and the Holy Roman Emperor in the 'Thirty Years War' and surrounded himself with Scottish advisors.

*Charles I and Henrietta Maria*

### Charles I (1625-1649)

Charles I was a very clever child. He was particularly good at languages, but he was also weak and sickly. He stuttered, had fits of rage and grew to only five feet four inches tall. Despite his problems he took to kingship with courage, dignity and seriousness. He married Henrietta Maria, who was a Catholic and the sister of King Louis XIII of France. During his reign he had to fight Catholic France and Spain and needed money to do this. Parliament would not agree to give him the money, so he paid for his unsuccessful wars by force and not paying his troops. He made peace in Europe, but upset the Scottish church when he tried to make all church services the same. He became even more unpopular because of the taxes he introduced and eventually war broke out between him and Parliament (see page 9). Charles was defeated by Parliament and was put on trial and executed.

*Charles II and his Portuguese wife, Catherine of Braganza*

### Charles II (1660-1685)

Charles II fought as a boy in the English Civil Wars, but eventually he had to flee to Holland. He travelled to Scotland in 1650 and was crowned King. He was nearly killed in his attempt to invade England with a Scottish army. After Cromwell's death Charles was welcomed back to England to take the throne. However, he was disliked because he entered into secret talks with France and fought a disastrous war against the Dutch. This war was begun in order to gain wealth and prestige. He had many mistresses, including an orange-seller called Nell Gwynne, who became a famous actress.

*James II and his second wife, Mary Modena*

## James II (1685-1688)

James had been captured during the Civil War, but he escaped to Holland disguised as a girl. He fought for the French and Spanish and was a brave soldier. He helped his brother Charles II rule and led the navy into battle against the Dutch. When it was discovered that he was a Catholic, Parliament decided that they did not like James and Charles took the decision to send him abroad. When James became King the disputes continued, especially when he put other Catholics into high places, like the army and navy and he arrested some Bishops. William of Orange was invited to come over from Holland to restore order and a Protestant throne, and he defeated James (see page 17).

*William III and Mary II*

## William and Mary (1688-1702)

William was married to Mary, James II's daughter. When Mary died of smallpox in 1694, William took over the throne and became William III. He was able to take over the throne without bloodshed.

> ### 🐇 Did You Know?
> For the first time, female roles in plays were played by women, instead of men dressed up as women. Nell Gwynne started her acting career by selling oranges at the theatre. 'Orange girls' were paid tips to pass messages between people in the audience. They often caught the eye of wealthy men. This is probably how Charles II first met Nell.

*Anne and her husband Prince George of Denmark, who was happy to let Anne rule on her own*

## Anne (1702-1714)

Anne was also James II's daughter and she had seventeen children, but they all died young. Despite being overweight and constantly in pain, she was a generous and hardworking queen. During her reign the Act of Union saw Scotland become united with England in 1707. When she died without an heir the throne passed to a German Prince called George, who was the first Hanoverian king.

> The costumes above were designed for King Charles I and his wife, Queen Henrietta Maria, to be worn in a 'masque'. The one on the left is for a knight. Masques were court plays which portrayed the monarchy in an idealised way and were nothing like real life. Design your own spectacular costumes for a masque.

4

# Daily Life

**Few people could find work on the land, as improved farming methods began to take over, so many people moved to the towns. Much of what we know about town life comes from the diaries people kept, the most famous belonging to Samuel Pepys who lived in London.**

### The Streets

Fires were common, as many of the building were wooden with thatched roofs. They were built close together, so fires spread quickly. The streets were narrow, crowded, noisy and disease-infested. People jostled to walk under the projecting upper rooms of houses, so that filth thrown from the windows did not land on top of them! Although there were rubbish collections, the roads were covered with dead dogs, cats and animal faeces. Houses had a cesspit, which was regularly emptied. There were sewers, but these were only for surface water.

### Personal Hygiene

The wool, or silken outer layers of clothes could not be washed and dry-cleaners did not exist. Most people had nits and lice and they stank, but this was normal, so nobody noticed! Those who could afford it would use scent. Hands and faces were washed several times a day. People cleaned their teeth with salt on their finger, or sulphuric acid on a piece of wood, but this eventually destroyed the enamel! Plaque was removed with little scrapers.

### Food

Breakfast was mainly for the wealthy and the main meal for most people was at lunchtime. The rich enjoyed meat, seafood, pies and tarts, but they did not eat many vegetables. Wine was drunk and sweetmeats and fruit were eaten for dessert. The poor ate mostly vegetables and oysters, which were cheap. Beer was drunk more than milk or water, as water was unsafe unless you bought it from a water-carrier. Water was obtained from a public well, or it was supplied to your home, but it was only good for cooking and washing. A light cold supper might be enjoyed by candlelight.

## Stuart Binge-drinkers!

Boys at Eton school had a daily allowance of beer and were punished if they did not drink it all. The sick at St Bartholomew's Hospital in London were entitled to three pints of beer.

### Entertainment

In London, if there wasn't a good execution to watch, people could visit the lunatic asylum at Bedlam to see the inmates. Bear and bull-baiting were popular and there was a zoo in the Tower of London. Other activities included walking in the royal parks, boat rides on the Thames, or trips to one of the new theatres. It was very fashionable to go to a coffee house, or for the poor, an alehouse.

### Appearance

Charles II made wig wearing for men fashionable, as well as the three-piece suit of knee breeches, waistcoat and a long jacket. Women still wore stiff corsets and long, bustling skirts. Men wore linen underwear, but women had no knickers. Artificial beauty spots shaped like moons, stars, suns, castles, birds and fishes were worn by ladies and gentlemen. A pale face was created using ceruse, which contained lead, so it poisoned the wearer! It also stank, cracked when you smiled and eventually turned a sinister grey colour!

### 🐭 Did You Know?

Bits of mouse skin were used to create higher eyebrows, their natural ones were plucked out. Rosy cheeks were created using cochineal, which is made from the dried bodies of small beetles.

### Medicine

Physicians used blood-letting to deal with most illnesses. The nearest equivalent to a chemist was an apothecary, who supplied remedies made of rare items such as the saliva of a fasting man, the moss which grew on an unburied skull, snails and woodlice! The local wise woman sold peculiar cures too. There were hospitals, but medical knowledge was very limited.

# A Stuart Home

Bare walls were no longer fashionable in the home. The only exception was in the kitchen, where the walls were lime washed annually. This improved the light and discouraged insects. Walls were painted in warm browns and sandy colours. Some walls were decorated with Biblical, or natural scenes and sometimes coats of arms. Painted cloth and wallpaper were available, often in very bright colours. Hanging tapestries were still popular. Furniture was influenced by continental designs.

Four-poster beds had curtains which could be drawn for warmth and privacy. This was especially important as underneath the bed there was room for a servant's folding bed. Before the use of calling bells, servants had to be near their masters and mistresses. Immovable, solid furniture gave way to elegant, lighter designs. Chamber pots continued to be used, as were 'close-stools', or padded boxes with a hole which contained a chamber pot. People spat all the time, so spittoons were everywhere! Globes of the world and the heavens were popular ornaments.

**Shops had large hanging signs nine feet from the ground to allow room for a man on a horse. Match these signs with their shop:**

| Sign | Shop |
|------|------|
| Adam and Eve | baskets |
| Cradle | ivory combs |
| Elephant | glazier |
| Cupid with a torch | apples and fruit |

**Design a hanging shop sign giving a clear clue about the product your shop is selling.**

Houses like the one on the left did not change much in the early Stuart period. They were still medieval in character and were made of local materials. They were 'E' or 'U' shaped. Later, houses like the one below were designed to show how important a family was, with ornate iron gates and a decorated porch. They were rectangular with sash windows. Larger houses had wings on either side.

**There are six things wrong with the picture above. See if you can find them.**

# The Gunpowder Plot

**English Catholics had suffered severe persecution during the end of Elizabeth I's reign, especially since the failed invasion by the Spanish Armada. Catholics were fined if they did not attend Protestant church services and James I was now anti-Catholic.**

### James Detests Catholics!
James had been sympathetic to Catholics. His wife was a Catholic, but two plots had been uncovered and he now needed the support of the Puritan nobility. So, he declared that he detested Catholicism and had all Jesuit and Catholic priests expelled.

### The Plotters
A Catholic nobleman called Robert Catesby had had enough. He had been heavily fined for hiding a Jesuit priest and for his part in a plot against Queen Elizabeth I. He had to sell his estates to pay the fines. He met with his friends Thomas Wintour, Jack Wright, Thomas Percy and a man called Guy Fawkes, who had served in the Spanish army. They discussed plans to blow up the King, Queen, government, judges, clergy and Protestant nobles when they met at the opening of Parliament.

### The Plan
Parliament had to be postponed for a month due to a plague, but this allowed the conspirators time to recruit more support. Thirty-six barrels of gunpowder were placed in a cellar, underneath the House of Lords. The idea was to destroy the King and government and then Fawkes would ask for help from foreign powers. The other plotters would then seize the King's daughter, Princess Elizabeth, and make her Queen.

### The Plot is Discovered!
A letter was sent to Catholic Lord Monteagle by one of the plotters and it warned him not to attend the opening of Parliament. Monteagle passed the letter to Robert Cecil, the Earl of Salisbury, who decided the best plan was to act at the last minute, catching the plotters in the act. Word managed to get back to the plotters that they had been betrayed, but they decided to proceed anyway. On the night of November 4th, 1605 Fawkes was discovered and the plot fell apart. The other conspirators fled in order to avoid capture.

> ## 🔖 Did You Know?
> To this day the Yeoman guards at Westminster conduct a ceremonial search before the State opening of Parliament. Nothing has ever been found.

### The Results of the Plot
Anti-Catholic feelings rose throughout the nation. New laws were passed preventing Catholics from practising the law, serving as army or navy officers and they were not allowed to vote in elections. Fear of Catholic or 'Popish' plots continued for a century. The King even wore padded clothes in case he was stabbed. The following year William Shakespeare created a play, called 'Macbeth', about the plot to murder a Scottish king.

### Could the Plot have Succeeded?
Due to the delay in opening Parliament the gunpowder had 'decayed' and the chemicals making it up had separated, rendering it useless. So, it would not have exploded. The large number of plotters meant that knowledge of the plot was more likely to leak out. Other countries did not want to lend their support to such a horrible plot and Catholics feared further persecution. Today, we celebrate 'Bonfire Night' when traditionally a stuffed 'Guy' is wheeled around to collect money for fireworks. The Guy is then burned on the bonfire.

## Punishment for Traitors!
Traitors were hung, drawn and quartered. They were dragged through London on a sledge and then hanged until half-dead. Next their body parts were cut off and burned in front of them. Whilst still alive their bowels and heart were removed. Finally, their heads were chopped off and their bodies were cut up into pieces and publicly displayed for the birds to eat their rotting flesh.

# Guy Fawkes is Captured!

Robert Cecil ordered Westminster to be searched on the evening of November 4th. The guards found only a cellar full of an unusually large amount of firewood. The King told Cecil to order a second search. This time Fawkes and the gunpowder were discovered in another cellar at around midnight.

The other plotters fled to the Midlands and hid in a house, but they were surrounded and many were killed in the fighting. Guy Fawkes was tortured for days before he eventually confessed to the details of the plot. He was hung, drawn and quartered with seven other plotters.

Can you find the powder flask, which was used to make a fuse?

# The English Civil War

**Charles I, like all Stuart monarchs, believed in the 'Divine Right of Kings'. He disliked the fact that he was not allowed to rule without Parliament's help. He summoned and dissolved Parliament three times before deciding to rule without it in 1629.**

### The Rift Between the King and Parliament

Thanks to his father, Charles inherited a country with money problems. He did not have the support of Parliament to raise money for his own expenses and wars, so he forced his nobles to give him loans. He put them in prison if they refused to pay. He demanded taxes without Parliament's agreement. When he tried to make changes to the Scottish church the Scots rebelled. Perhaps if he had been less rigid in his demands and more willing to compromise he might not have faced so much opposition.

### Parliament is Divided

Charles needed money to fight the Scots, so he summoned Parliament in 1640. He had to agree to certain demands before they agreed to help him. Some MP's thought his demands had gone too far, but a group formed to support Charles. When a Catholic revolt broke out in Ireland, Parliament did not want to give Charles an army, fearing that he might turn on them, so they put the army under their own control. The King was furious. He entered Parliament with soldiers hoping to arrest five MP's, but they had already fled. The year was 1642. Charles's supporters, the 'Royalists', left Parliament and followed him.

### The Nation is Divided

The split between Royalists and Parliamentarians left many families and friends divided. Catholics supported the King, but most Protestants and Puritans were on Parliament's side. Charles had support in the north and west, whilst Parliament had control of the richer south-east. Scotland changed sides on several occasions during the war. Foreign soldiers arrived to fight not for a cause, but for pay and 'handsome English women'! Charles's reliance on foreign troops lost him support at home.

### 🐎 Did You Know?

As the war progressed volunteers became harder to find. They were taken from the unemployed, criminals and the homeless. These men often deserted just before or during a battle.

### The First Civil War 1642-1646

The King set up his base at Oxford, but he wanted to capture London. The first major battle was fought at Edgehill in Warwickshire in 1642, but neither side won. At the Battle of Marston Moor in 1644 Charles's nephew, Prince Rupert was defeated. The following year the King was beaten at the Battle of Naseby by the 'New Model Army' (see page 12). The King's army surrendered and he fled to Scotland.

### The Second Civil War 1647-1648

Oliver Cromwell (see page 11) stopped a Welsh revolt, but then the Scots attacked. They were defeated even though Cromwell was outnumbered two to one. The rest of the Royalists were beaten by the commander of the Parliamentary army, Sir Thomas Fairfax. Fairfax was nearly killed in a street battle at Torrington in Devon, when the Royalist gunpowder stores in the church exploded, showering debris everywhere.

### Cromwell Comes to Power

Cromwell had tried to make a deal with Charles, but when the King continued to rebel he felt he had no choice but to hunt him down. Charles was tried for treason in 1649 and was beheaded at Whitehall. He still believed to his last breath in the 'Divine Right of Kings'. With Ireland and most of Scotland under English rule, the nation was now a republic, or 'Commonwealth'. The monarchy and the House of Lords were abolished, but there was a lot of quarrelling among different factions now that the King had gone. Cromwell tried to give power to 140 devout churchmen, but this failed. He was head of the army and the obvious choice to take power. Eventually he was made Lord Protector in 1653. He died in 1658 and his son succeeded him, but Richard Cromwell, or 'Tumbledown Dick', as he was known, was forced to resign. The nation was to be ruled by a king once more.

# Cavaliers and Roundheads

There wasn't an army standing, so armies were raised from apprentices, labourers and farmers who had to supply their own weapons. Officers wore coloured sashes or a 'gorget', which was a piece of neck armour, to show their rank. The supporters of the King came to be known as 'cavaliers', which was really an insult, as the real meaning was colourful playboys. They called the Parliamentary army 'roundheads', referring to the very short hair of the working class London apprentices. The roundheads generally dressed more plainly and did not have long hair in ringlets like the cavaliers.

## Navy versus Castles

Parliament had control of the navy, which was a great advantage because they could resupply their army quickly. The Royalists had control of many castles. They had garrisons at Sudeley, Nunney, Tamworth, Donnington and Banbury Castle. Pembroke Castle was held by Parliamentarian troops, but because they weren't paid, they changed sides! Cromwell successfully besieged Pembroke by cutting off the water supply, then he had the castle dismantled.

A typical battle would start with a bombardment by the artillery (below). The infantry was made up of musketeers and pikemen. Some were as young as thirteen years of age. The pikeman below is ready to defend against cavalry with a pike over 4.5 metres long.

**Women in War**
*Few wives went with their husbands to war, but women 'camp followers' did accompany the baggage train. They earned their food by washing, sewing, cooking and tending to the wounded. If food was scarce, the soldiers were fed first.*

**The New Model Army**
*The 'New Model Army' was the beginning of the British army. For the first time soldiers were paid regular wages, received standard equipment and uniforms and were given proper training. Officers were promoted based on their abilities, not on their social status.*

# Oliver Cromwell

**Oliver Cromwell was born in 1599 in Huntingdon, Cambridgeshire. At the age of 18 he had to look after his family and their farm after the death of his father. He took an active role in local government and became a Member of Parliament in 1628.**

Cromwell fought for reforms to give Parliament more power. At the start of the Civil War he led a cavalry unit and rose through the ranks very quickly. He fought bravely at the head of his troops and at one battle was wounded in the head. Eventually he was made second in command under Sir Thomas Fairfax. He won a significant victory at the Battle of Naseby.

## Cromwell's Religious Beliefs

Cromwell was driven by his faith and felt he was doing God's will. He was a Puritan, which was a term of ridicule for people who wanted to 'purify' the church. The Puritans aimed to remove all of the religious trappings from the church, including statues, all pomp and ceremony and returning to a simple form of worship. Some disliked the church so much that they emigrated to North America. One such group were the 'Pilgrim Fathers' who sailed in a ship called the Mayflower.

## The Irish and Scots Rebel

Cromwell was sent to Ireland, as they had rebelled in support of the Royalists in 1649. He brutally put down the revolt and thousands of Irish Catholics were massacred. Many Protestants, who wanted revenge for an earlier massacre in Ulster by Catholics, saw the Irish as savages. Cromwell put many of his men in charge of Irish lands. Many Irish people were mistreated and sent abroad as slaves. The Scots proclaimed Charles I's son as King and he became King Charles II and invaded in the name of the 'Jacobite', or Stuart cause. Cromwell beat them at the Battle of Dunbar, but Charles went on to capture London. He was defeated at the Battle of Worcester and fled to France. This was the last time Parliament fought the King. Cromwell returned to London in triumph.

## The Protectorate

Cromwell was now Lord Protector of England, Scotland and Ireland. He started signing his name 'Oliver P', in the same way monarchs had signed their names, such as 'Elizabeth R'. Although he was offered the crown he refused it, but people called him 'Your Highness.' In 1653 Cromwell dismissed Parliament, because they did not support his reforms. He tried to divide England and Wales under the command of fifteen of his officers, but this did not last. He wanted to make the country prosper by inviting Jews, who had helped the Dutch economy, to England. Although he ruled with an iron fist, there was generally freedom of religion. However, after five years he was dead.

## The Restoration of the Monarchy

In 1660, Parliament sent for King Charles II to rule. Cromwell's body was dug up and beheaded on the same day as Charles I's execution. His head was displayed on a pole outside Westminster Abbey. Those who had signed Charles I's death warrant were executed. Others fled, or begged for forgiveness. The army was disbanded. Under Charles II, who was known as the 'merry monarch', the nation enjoyed a period of peace. Theatres, which had been closed by the Puritans, were reopened. The King strengthened the Church of England and passed laws discriminating against Catholics and anyone who opposed the church. He was supported by the new Tory party, which had formed in Parliament. An opposition party had also formed called the Whigs. The fact that the King was relying on a group of men to help him govern, meant that the government was very similar to the system we know today.

> **If you had to choose between supporting the King or Parliament, who would you choose and why? Would you be able to fight your own family, friends or neighbour? This is the situation many people had to face in the Civil War.**

# The Battle of Naseby 1645

*Sir Thomas Fairfax decided to besiege the King's capital of Oxford with his New Model Army. Outnumbered by two to one, the King wanted to lure Fairfax away from Oxford and deployed his army of 7,500 men near Naseby. His nephew Prince Rupert saw some Parliamentarian scouts riding away and thought it was the enemy retreating. He led a fierce cavalry charge, but in chasing the opposing side he and his men had left the battlefield! The other Royalists marched forward, but when they went over a ridge they realised the size of the army they were facing.*

*On the opposite side, Cromwell led his cavalry in a victorious charge. In the centre of the battle, after an exchange of musket fire, the opposing infantries clashed with pikes and close-quarter fighting. However, the Parliamentarians began falling back, so Fairfax led his reserves into battle, whilst Cromwell and his cavalry charged at the Royalists rear. The King was about to charge bravely with his reserves, but he was stopped by the Earl of Carnwath, who asked "Will you go upon your death?" The King fled and his army surrendered.*

*Above, Cromwell leads a cavalry charge at Naseby*

## 🐎 Did You Know?
**Cromwell has more roads named after him than any other English person, with the exception of Queen Victoria.**

# The Great Plague

**The last major outbreak of plague in Europe killed at least twenty million people during the Middle Ages. It then reappeared at regular intervals until the next big outbreak in 1665. The 'Great Plague of London' killed about 110,000 people.**

### A Prosperous City

In 1665, London's population stood at about 350,000, the largest in Europe and second only to Paris. Property prices were high and people were building on every available piece of land. Foreigners set up their businesses in this flourishing city, which was now an important financial centre in Europe. It was also a centre of entertainment, with theatres and playhouses, which had been re-opened after the return of the monarchy.

The only bridge across the River Thames was London Bridge. It had houses and shops on it, some of which were six storeys high. Some upper storeys met across the street. The river was full of boats, such as the water taxis or 'skiffs' and 'wherries', which were river buses. These were faster than Hackney carriages, which often became stuck in traffic jams. The city had a postal service and at night the streets were lit.

### Conditions Ripe for a Plague

In 1603 and 1625, 70,000 people had already died from plague in London, with thousands more dying in the intervening years. It was a dirty, overcrowded city with very wealthy merchants and bankers living next to the very poor. The cobbled streets were full of horse-drawn coaches and carts, street sellers and rubbish. It was swarming with rats and London was experiencing an uncomfortable heat wave.

### Emergency Laws Introduced

When the plague struck, the Mayor of London ordered emergency measures. Watchmen guarded infected houses to keep people locked inside. Dead bodies were checked for infection and arrangements were made for the disposal of rubbish. Forty thousand dogs were killed by appointed animal killers. Plague-infected houses were marked with a red cross.

### Samuel Pepys

In his diary, Samuel Pepys tells us that he stopped wearing his new wig, or 'periwig', in case it had been made from the hair of a dead plague victim! He also says that the King left London, along with many wealthy families and that 'grass grows all up and down Whitehall.' Shops, taverns and theatres were closed. Fairs and sports were banned and everyone had to be indoors by nine o'clock in the evening. However, bakers were ordered to keep baking. The boatmen left with their families and thousands of houses became empty as people fled. The river and streets were deserted and this must have been a strange sight in such a busy city.

### Cures

People thought that burning herbs, smoking tobacco, or taking snuff would protect them from the plague. Most doctors left London, but the ones who remained wore protective clothing, including a beaked mask stuffed with herbs, but they did not have the medical knowledge to help victims. Many people bought magic charms from pedlars, believing that they would protect them from the plague.

### What is Plague?

The plague was probably bubonic plague and it is believed that it was spread by fleas carried on black rats. It may have reached London on board Dutch trading ships, which carried bales of cotton from Amsterdam. Today, there are no black rats in Europe as the bigger brown rats have replaced them. There are still outbreaks of plague around the world, but now there is a cure. 'Bubonic' comes from the Greek word for groin and this is where large swellings first appeared in plague victims. Plague victims would ache, sweat, vomit, cough up blood and suffer from diarrhoea. Pus-filled 'buboes' appeared and death followed within three days.

# "Bring Out Your Dead!"

*A plague bell rang and alerted people to the arrival of the corpse bearers, who took away bodies during the night. The graveyards were full, so the dead were thrown into grave pits, which held thirty to forty bodies.*

## A Village's Sacrifice

Towns and villages outside London were also affected. Perhaps the most famous was the village of Eyam in Derbyshire. The plague arrived with a merchant carrying a parcel of cloth sent from London. The 350 villagers selflessly isolated themselves to stop the disease from spreading. Two hundred and sixty of them died and you can still see their graves today.

# The Great Fire of London

**No sooner had the plague devastated London than the city was suddenly engulfed in fire. The flames were driven by the wind and a fire storm swept across the tightly packed wooden houses and continued to burn for five days.**

In the early hours of 2nd September, 1666 a fire started at the house of Thomas Farynor, the King's baker, in Pudding Lane near London Bridge. The Farynor family fled across the roofs leaving a frightened maid who was consumed in the flames. The Lord Mayor of London was slow to respond to the emergency, but the King ordered him to demolish homes to stop the fire spreading. The strong winds meant that this had little effect. Fortunately, the Tower of London garrison successfully created firebreaks by destroying some buildings with gunpowder and the winds died down slowing the fires' progress. A break in the houses on London Bridge, caused by a previous fire, halted the fires' progress south of the river. The Duke of York was ordered to take control of the situation and with the help of the militia stopped looters.

## The Destruction of London
The lead on St Paul's Cathedral melted and ran down Ludgate Hill. A third of the city was destroyed including 13,200 houses, 44 company halls, 84 churches and many river boats. Fortunately, not many people died, although it was probably more than the official death toll of four people.

## The Aftermath of the Fire
Many of the people made homeless camped outside the old medieval walls of the city. Some went back to the country, whilst others managed to find homes in the city. Merchants and tradesmen had been ruined when their businesses went up in smoke. They did not have fire insurance at that time.

## Conspiracy Theories
People attacked Roman Catholics, believing the fire was a Popish plot to take control of England. They also attacked French and Dutch people and the King's guard even stooped to assaulting people who spoke poor English! King Charles addressed 100,000 people who had been made homeless and told them the fire was an act of God and not a foreign plot. They were not convinced.

## A Parliamentary Committee Investigates
During an investigation by Parliament a French Protestant watchmaker, Robert Hubert, confessed to starting the fire at the bakery with 23 conspirators. This confession contained errors and the judges did not believe his story, but members of the baker's family were some of those sitting on the jury. Hubert was hanged. A monument to the fire had an inscription blaming 'the treachery and malice of the Popish faction', until it was finally removed in 1831.

## A New City Rises From the Ashes
Sir Christopher Wren was part of a team appointed to oversee the rebuilding of the city. Ambitious plans for a complete reconstruction of London were rejected. Instead a less dramatic change was agreed to be the quickest way forward. Brick houses were built according to new laws, replacing the old rat-infested wooden houses. Streets were widened and sometimes straightened and alleys were made bigger. By 1676 virtually all of the destroyed city had been rebuilt. Sir Christopher Wren designed 51 new churches, as well as St Paul's Cathedral with its magnificent dome. This is still a well known feature of the London skyline today.

*Firemen using a tub-type fire engine, whilst another fireman pulls down a burning building with a long hook.*

# Pirates and Highwaymen

Gallows were a common site at crossroads and the swinging bodies of criminals acted as a warning. Highwaymen, or 'gentlemen of the road' held up coaches and robbed travellers. The most notorious highwayman of them all was Dick Turpin, who swung from the gallows in 1739. He was a burglar, smuggler, horse thief and murderer. Smuggling was a big problem. Taxes on imported goods were so high that smugglers would bring brandy, tobacco and silk ashore without paying the tax. Piracy was rife, but it was generally ignored, as long as the pirates attacked foreign ships. When they started raiding British vessels they were hunted down. Edward Teach, known as 'Blackbeard', was shot and beheaded in 1718. Two female pirates, Mary Read and Anne Bonny, escaped hanging in Jamaica, as they were both pregnant.

## The Wicked Lady!

It was not only men who were highway robbers, but sometimes well-bred women. Katherine Ferrers may have been the 'Wicked Lady' who terrorised Nomansland Common in Hertfordshire. Apart from robbery, she burned houses, slaughtered livestock and even committed murder. She is said to have died of gunshot wounds during a robbery which went wrong.

*Katherine Ferrers points her pistols at the coach, as her partner in crime, Ralph Chaplin steals from the passengers.*

16

# William of Orange

**Charles II died in 1685 leaving a strong monarchy. His Catholic brother James II came to the throne and managed to make a lot of enemies. He suspended anti-Catholic laws and gave Catholics positions in the army and government.**

### The Bloody Assizes

The Protestant Duke of Monmouth, an illegitimate son of Charles II, landed in Dorset. He tried to seize the throne, but he was beaten at Sedgemoor. He and many of his supporters were executed, whilst others were sold as slaves. They were so ruthlessly treated that the trials were known as the 'Bloody' Assizes.

### The Glorious Revolution

James imprisoned those who opposed him, or removed them from important positions. The King had the support of the Tories, but when his second wife gave birth to a son, they realised that the heir to the throne would be a Catholic. The Tory and Whig parties secretly contacted James's son-in-law, the Dutch Prince William of Orange. William landed at Torbay in Devon in 1688 and advanced to London. James fled to France when his supporters deserted him. This became known as 'The Glorious Revolution'.

### Parliament Passes the Bill of Rights

Parliament offered the crown to William and Mary. In return they re-introduced the laws which had been suspended under James II. These gave Parliament more power and limited the King's authority. With the passing of the Bill of Rights, Parliament became the supreme law-making body. Catholics were not allowed to sit on the throne. William did not oppose Parliament, as he wanted their help to stand against France and the Jacobites. A more practical tax system was created to fund the monarchy, government and foreign affairs, including wars.

### A Dutch King

William was asthmatic and slightly hunchbacked, but well educated, a master of languages and a good soldier. He learned to be a soldier whilst fighting the French, who had occupied the Netherlands. With Spanish and Austrian help, he organised resistance against the French and drove them out of his homeland.

### Mary

Mary was a pretty fifteen year old who had been brought up in the Church of England. William married her to gain English support in his war against the French King Louis XIV. Mary died of smallpox in 1694 at the age of thirty-three. William never remarried and his popularity faded until his death in 1702.

> ### 🔖 Did You Know?
> When William landed in England he told the crowd, "I come to do you goot; I am here for all your goots."

### William's Battles

In 1689, James II went to Dublin in Ireland to try to regain the throne. A year later, William defeated his father-in-law James at the Battle of the Boyne, a victory which is still celebrated in Northern Ireland today by Protestant 'Orangemen'. He added Ireland, Scotland and England to his Spanish and Austrian allies to create a 'Grand Alliance' against France. He spent the next few years in Europe, personally fighting the French to protect his Dutch homeland. Unlike previous kings, he co-operated with Parliament and received the money he needed for his wars. He was so intent on fighting the French that he made sure there were no problems at home. This meant he was a very tolerant King and the nation enjoyed religious and political freedom under his rule.

## Massacre at Glencoe

In 1692, William granted an amnesty to Scottish clans who swore an oath of loyalty to him, but the chief of the MacDonald clan of Glencoe was late in responding to the amnesty. Troops went to Glencoe under the command of a Campbell, an old enemy of the MacDonalds, although they were now related by marriage. The troops were shown hospitality by the Macdonalds, but were brutally murdered in their own homes. Thirty-eight men were killed and forty women and children died of exposure after their homes were burned.

# The Battle of the Boyne 1690

*William arrived in Ulster in June with 16,000 foreign troops to add to the 20,000 already in Ireland. His foreign troops were better armed and more experienced than James's men. The Jacobite army was smaller, with about 23,000 troops. Some were from France, but many were Irish Catholic peasants. William marched to Dublin, whilst James set up a line of defence on the south side of the Boyne River, about 50km from Dublin.*

*On the 1st of July the Williamite army successfully crossed a ford after some fierce fighting and they secured control of a village. Much of the fighting happened in the river as William's troops tried to cross it at several points. They were able to fend off successive cavalry attacks and eventually caused the Jacobites to retreat, but it was not a decisive victory. The death toll was quite low and the bulk of the Irish army continued to resist English rule. However, James had given up and fled to France in a panic, whilst hopes of a Jacobite rising in Scotland faded too.*

# The Arts & Sciences

**The 17th century was a time when scientific knowledge made great leaps and there was a blossoming of new philosophical ideas, literature, art and architecture.**

## The Royal Society

King Charles II founded the Royal Observatory at Greenwich to observe the sun, moon, stars and planets to aid the navigation of ships. It was built by Sir Christopher Wren, who was an astronomer before he was an architect. The first Astronomers Royal, Edmund Halley and John Flamsteed, were members of the Royal Society of London, which was founded in 1660 to encourage learning. Other members included Samuel Pepys, Isaac Newton, Robert Hooke and Robert Boyle.

## Isaac Newton 1643-1727

Isaac Newton was a brilliant mathematician and became one of the greatest scientists in the world. He invented the reflecting telescope, which advanced our knowledge of the solar system. A reflecting telescope uses mirrors rather than lenses, which avoids the problem of light refraction. Newton studied light, discovering that white light could be separated into colours and that it is made up of particles. He also developed a theory of gravity from his observations of planetary orbits.

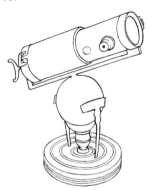

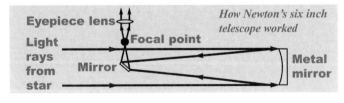

How Newton's six inch telescope worked

Eyepiece lens

Light rays from star

Focal point

Mirror

Metal mirror

## Robert Hooke 1635-1703

Robert Hooke, who accused Newton of not giving him credit for his work on gravity, wrote the first book on microscopic studies. His other achievements included numerous mechanical devices, such as the universal joint, which is used in all motor cars today. He also studied the properties of gases.

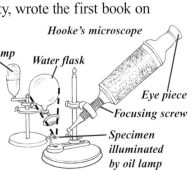

Hooke's microscope

Oil lamp

Water flask

Eye piece

Focusing screw

Specimen illuminated by oil lamp

## Robert Boyle 1627-1691

Irish physicist and chemist Robert Boyle discovered various laws of physics, which were named after him.

## Edmund Halley 1656-1742

Halley's Comet is named after the English mathematician and astronomer Edmund Halley. In 1680 he accurately predicted the return of the comet bearing his name every 76 years.

## William Harvey 1578-1657

William Harvey revolutionised medical thought on the functions of parts of the human body. This contributed to modern surgery techniques. He also discovered the circulatory system of blood.

## Philosophy

Thomas Hobbes believed that individual freedoms need to be controlled and directed for the good of the many, and this is best done by the monarchy. John Locke wrote about the mind and suggested that our beliefs must be based on experiment. He greatly influenced later philosophy and the American revolutionaries fighting against British rule.

## Poetry

John Milton wrote 'Paradise Lost' in 1667. It was about the Biblical fall of man and the conflict between the will of God and free will, relating it to his disappointment in the politics of his day. Metaphysical poets like John Donne, George Herbert and Andrew Marvell were influenced by Greek philosophy, which asked questions about the meaning of life and what reality is. Their poems often used images taken from new scientific discoveries.

## Painting

Flemish painters Peter Paul Rubens and Anthony van Dyck came to the court of Charles I. Van Dyck painted many pictures of the King, making his small stature seem impressive and dignified.

## Music

Henry Purcell wrote the first English opera in 1689 and he is one of Britain's greatest composers.

# St Paul's Cathedral

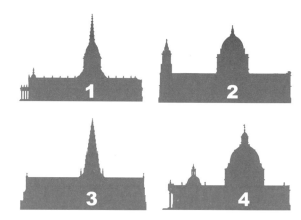

*In 1668, Christopher Wren was still only in his thirties and was asked to re-design St Paul's Cathedral, which had been destroyed by the Great Fire. It took him ten years to design and forty years to build. Another famous architect, Inigo Jones, had added classical architecture to the original St Paul's. Until then churches were built in a medieval style. Wren came up with a 'Great Model' with a huge dome at the centre, but the clergy rejected it, favouring the more traditional cross design. Wren was very disappointed and came up with another design. The 'Warrant' design was medieval in shape, but classical in style, without such a large dome. It was approved by Charles II, who allowed Wren some freedom to make changes, which the architect fully exploited. Hidden behind screen walls a vastly altered building emerged and the large dome reappeared. Although it was not the design Wren had originally intended, it was still a magnificent achievement.*

**Match the silhouettes of St Paul's above to their correct names below:**

| | |
|---|---|
| *Medieval St Paul's* | number _____ |
| *The Great Model* | number _____ |
| *The Warrant design* | number _____ |
| *The final design* | number _____ |

**Design your own idea for a cathedral. It can be modern in style, or based on medieval or Roman architecture.**

**1** *The stone lantern is supported by a brick cone inside the dome. This is hidden by a false dome ceiling inside, which is decorated with paintings.*
**2** *There are 530 steps to the Golden Gallery.*
**3** *The world's second largest dome, after St Peter's in Rome, is made of timber covered in lead.*
**4** *The entrance to the crypt, which contains the tombs of Wren, Lord Nelson and the Duke of Wellington.*
**5** *The main entrance at the west end.*

# Giant Stuart Word Search

| G | A | E | N | G | L | I | S | H | C | I | V | I | L | W | A | R | S | O | M |
|---|---|---|---|---|---|---|---|---|---|---|---|---|---|---|---|---|---|---|---|
| R | N | T | O | L | P | R | E | D | W | O | P | N | U | G | H | O | Q | A | R |
| E | S | T | U | A | R | T | V | R | I | I | E | N | N | Y | L | U | R | H | W |
| A | P | E | R | I | W | I | G | R | O | U | O | O | A | I | L | Y | U | N | I |
| T | T | A | S | E | U | Q | S | A | G | U | D | I | V | A | Q | R | D | Y | L |
| F | N | L | A | C | T | U | S | A | S | N | N | E | R | U | C | A | R | R | L |
| I | E | S | D | N | A | N | L | O | O | R | R | D | E | I | J | P | B | A | I |
| R | M | U | A | M | S | P | L | L | E | C | E | E | H | A | T | I | N | M | A |
| E | A | T | M | N | T | F | F | N | R | H | N | I | N | E | L | N | G | D | M |
| O | I | T | R | A | O | O | N | O | T | O | H | E | L | L | A | U | I | N | O |
| F | L | I | E | R | R | A | M | A | F | R | M | G | O | A | Y | D | S | A | F |
| L | R | R | S | E | N | W | C | S | A | Y | A | F | R | F | V | E | S | M | O |
| O | G | W | W | E | E | S | C | C | A | N | R | I | A | M | O | A | I | A | R |
| N | P | O | E | L | L | O | A | W | B | I | A | W | T | R | L | S | C | I | A |
| D | T | U | L | U | T | R | H | E | G | O | K | T | E | O | E | A | C | L | N |
| O | Q | S | A | S | O | G | A | H | D | E | R | B | I | M | R | C | E | L | G |
| N | U | P | L | A | I | H | T | H | S | T | O | N | A | R | U | R | T | I | E |
| N | T | L | O | H | D | S | M | A | C | Y | H | J | N | E | U | L | E | W | N |
| S | A | M | U | E | L | P | E | P | Y | S | E | N | I | R | E | P | T | E | C |
| W | E | S | T | E | N | Y | O | B | E | H | T | F | O | E | L | T | T | A | B |

| | | | | |
|---|---|---|---|---|
| Stuart | William of Orange | Puritan | Guy Fawkes | Samuel Pepys |
| Gunpowder Plot | James I | Mary Queen of Scots | Cavaliers | Highwaymen |
| Great Fire of London | Charles II | Beer | Roundheads | Battle of the Boyne |
| Great Plague | Queen Anne | Tower of London | Oliver Cromwell | Bill of Rights |
| English Civil War | William and Mary | Traitor | Periwig | St Pauls Cathedral |